This Too Shall Pass

Healing the Hurt

Dr. Yvonne Henderson

This Too Shall Pass

Healing the Hurt

This Too Shall Pass: Healing the Hurt
Copyright ©2022 Transitions Publishing

All rights reserved by the author. No one part of this book may be reproduced in any form without the permission of the author.

Scripture quotations are taken from the New King James Version (NKJV) copyright © 1982-2006 by Thomas Nelson, Inc.

Emphasis within the scripture quotations is the author's own, all pronouns used to refer to God will be capitalized. The name of Satan and related references are not capitalized intentionally.

Printed in the United States of America

Published by Transitions Publishing
Missouri City, Texas 77489
Transitionspublishing@gmail.com
www.dryvonnehenderson.com

Prelude
(Introduction to Deliver Me by Donald Lawrence)

He leads me beside still waters, He restoreth my soul. When you become a believer, your spirit is made right and sometimes the soul doesn't get the notice, it has a hole in it, due to things that has happened in the past, hurt, abuse, molestation. But we want to speak to you today and tell you, that God wants to heal the hole in your soul. Some peoples' actions are not because their spirit was wrong, but it is because the past has left a hole in their soul. May this wisdom help you get over your past and remind you that God wants to heal the hole in your soul.

Dedication

This book is for those who have been hurt by family, friends, churches and even themselves. This is a snippet of my testimony to let you know there is healing after this, there is freedom after this. As I began to heal, and close the hole in my soul, God showed me the people who needed this just as much as I did. I pray that you will find comfort in the scriptures and messages you are about to read to help you heal from your hurt and close the hole in your own soul.

Dr. Yvonne Henderson

Table of Contents

Prelude ii

Dedication iii

Introduction 1

Healing The Hurt 8

Steps To Healing 20

How To Face Your Fears 33

Relevance After Rejection 47

How To Build 55

Victory Is Mine 65

My Brother's Keeper 76

Time To Go 89

Postlude 97

Introduction

Life for the most part can be hard enough without having others to project their expectations on you. In my 50+ years I have had to deal with the expectations of others and what they thought about me and how I should live my life. It took a while for me to learn that I only had one life to live, and I needed to live my life. I cannot nor can you live life for someone else.

In life I have seen how parents project their dreams onto their children to make them what they failed to become. It is okay to have hopes and dreams for your children, but let it be their hopes and dreams and not yours. Often, we do not realize we are projecting our hopes and dreams on our children and what it creates in the process. Children begin to resent their parents and rebel, or worse.

I had to come to that realization with my son, when I was trying to get him to finish high school and go on to college. I can remember saying he was lazy and just wanted to play video games, and one day he told me the reason he didn't do anything was because I said he would not do anything. What I thought was reverse psychology backfired on me. I thought I could project my thoughts of him finishing high school and going to college by using the tactics used on me. Well, I was different, if someone told me I could not do something I did my best to prove them wrong. That did not work on my son, because what I said, made him not want to do any better because I did not expect anything better out of him. I had to talk to him to see what he wanted and realized he did not want to follow in my footsteps and go on the college and get a doctorate and guess what? I had to be okay with that. It was not his hope or dream to go off to college and get higher level degrees like I did. As a result of me pushing there were a lot of hurtful things that were said and done on both sides of the coin. Raising my child from age 10 until now has been one of the

most difficult moments in my life. You may ask why? Because during these last 10 years I had to face some of my strongest demons and strongholds to help me break through into my freedom. I had to deal with the things that had hurt me, that I had not dealt with. I went through a healing process that only God could have delivered me from. Some things I had swept under the rug, so to speak came to the surface and my son was able to point some of them out to me. I was hurt at first, but then God spoke and said, "Had those words come from anyone else you would not have received them. I used him because I knew you would listen." Thus began my journey to healing the hurt that had been caused in my life. I had to deal with inner hurt that I had caused myself by my negative self-talk over the years. I had to deal with hurt from others in the form of betrayal from some of the closest people to me. I had to deal with being a victim of molestation, and rape not once, but twice. This hurt showed up in my relationships and how I selected a mate.

When my son pointed out some things to me, I had to deal with them even though it hurt. I had to deal with the loss of my parents, the hurt I felt and had never dealt with, let's look.

Reflections

Healing The Hurt

Even though you may have to cry sometimes, you won't have to cry always, God is going to wipe every tear from your eyes. I can't count how many times I have cried myself to sleep over people who have hurt me. I was told once that my tears were a part of the healing process and every time, I cry God is healing a hurt. I tell you He has healed a lot of hurt, because I have cried a many of tears over the years.

I really needed to hear that because for a long time I had gotten to a place where I either didn't want to or couldn't cry. I had

become so numb to the pain by doing other things I could not cry. God
revealed to me through my Godson, Prophet Bryan O'Neil, that my tears were going to be a part of my healing. He said, "Every tear would literally become an issue that was being healed," He also said, "Every time you cry, just say thank You Lord for healing me." As I cried it began to release my healing through my voice, I spoke to the healing taking place in my soul. I can say that over the last three years God has healed me and allowed me to write this book to show you what He did.

When you are hurting, it is hard to develop and form healthy relationships. Sometimes our relationships are not healthy because of what we have been exposed to. Growing up, I saw how my dad treated my mom, at the beginning it was great because I was so young, I did not know what I was looking for. As I grew up, I saw that my dad could be abusive due the Post Traumatic Stress Disorder (PTSD) developed as a result of him being in the Vietnam War. Don't get it twisted, he loved my mom, but there were some incidents of verbal and physical abuse that I can recall along with him cheating, that shaped my thoughts on relationships as a young girl of what I did not want in a marriage to the point that I said I did not want to be in a relationship or get married. As I got older, I saw that through it all my mom and dad stayed together and worked through what was happening.

I began to go to church at age 18, at which time I was still a virgin and had no intention on having sex with anyone anytime soon. At the church I was taught that you had to wait until marriage to have sex or it was a sin. I was fine with that because it was not a part of my agenda anyway. I can recall making a pack (covenant) with two other young ladies in the church, that we would not have sex until we were married, and we would hold each other accountable. Well, time went on and the other two had found love, or so I thought, got married and started a family. Well needless to say after doing the right thing, they both were separated and divorced after a couple of years of marriage, due to mental and/or emotional abuse. At this time, I too was beginning to embark on a new relationship that I thought would lead to marriage, until the unfortunate happened, my finance' was discharged from the military with a dishonorable discharge due to preexisting medical reasons. I was floored, I had to return the ring because it wasn't being paid for and he had moved back to Atlanta. Trying to be a good woman, I traveled to Atlanta on our scheduled wedding date February 14, 1986, that had been cancelled because of his condition, only to be surprised by him being with another women, whom he said had been there by his side to take care of him when I wasn't. I was hurt, hence started my downward spiral. I then thought, "What's the sense in waiting, if it's only going to end up like this?" From that point I vowed never to get married. I was not really concerned about having kids, since I said I would adopt, if I did not have any by age 29.

Another relationship ensued, oh I thought this was the one, he was the Minister of Music at a church in Chicago, where I had visited, and he inquired about me, and it was set up. I visited him in Chicago on several occasions and then it happened, he wanted sex. Still a virgin at age 21 I said, "But you are the whole Minister of Music, you know that isn't right." He replied, "I'm a man too and I have needs." I was petrified and confused,
because he was a man of God and was to uphold the ordinances of God, what do I do? He assured me it would not hurt, so it happened. Our first time was not vaginal it was oral, it was an amazing experience I

would never forget. Then he showed me the membrane that lined my vagina and said, "this is your cherry you are no longer a virgin." The next time we got tougher he wanted to have intercourse, that was the most painful experience I had ever had. Even though he went slow I still cried because of the pain. Even though I did not enjoy it we keep doing it.

Some time passed, and he was up for a pastoral position, I supported and went with him on assignments, I helped with his studies, and he said we were going to get married. I though, "Wow! I'm going to be a first lady." It was scary and exciting at the same time. Well, the time came for his installation service, I went and was ushered to sit in the back of the church. When service was over there was a fellowship dinner and I wasn't invited. His mother was there, and he introduced me as a friend. I'm thinking, "a friend, the woman that just ironed your clothes, and curled your toes, but I'm just a friend." This was it, I was crushed, I picked up my heart and went home. I called, with no response, after some time, he called and informed me that he did not think I was first lady material and we had to part ways. WOW!

I became very promiscuous, sleeping around with different partners trying to heal the hurt I was feeling, the feeling of not being loved by those of the opposite sex. You may think, I did not have a male figure in my life to guide me, but I did. My father was always there for me. He told me how beautiful and great I was, he built my self-esteem to the point I did not need a man to tell me those things, but something was still lacking. He had never told me how to have a relationship with a man and what to look for in a good man. So, I went out in search of what one was.

As I tried to grow, I found myself being pulled

in yet another destructive direction. After years of self-destructive behavior Holy Spirit spoke to me and said, "Come home. It's time to deal with the pain, so the Father can use you, you're ready." I felt like the protocol son, I had gone out so far, and done so much, I had hit rock bottom and did not think God still loved me. Holy Spirit said, "He does." At that moment I knew He had been calling me and I had been running. After answering my calling to preach, God gave me a series of sermons to help heal the hurt. He said for me to reach the people I had to heal first. So, during my healing process these sermons were birthed, and I pray they help you heal.

Reflections

Steps to Healing

Step One: God will separate you from who's hurting you. According to Psalms 6:8-10 (vs, 8) says, "depart from me all workers of iniquity, now we have got to understand what is being said. Iniquities are done in the dark, it's going on behind closed doors. See we have got to stop walking around during the day acting like everything is okay when you are in turmoil, you must confront your hurt not protect it. What is hurting you in secret? You do not have to answer that right now, just think about it. Who is someone you can talk to and be honest with? God will put people in your life after you have departed from the wrong ones to help you get on track.

    An accountability partner is necessary, because if you are not accountable to anyone you will do anything. I know this to be true from experience. When I was out in the world doing me, I did not hold myself accountable to anyone and I found myself doing things I did not think I would ever do. I was racking up notches on my belt, not listening to anyone, I was like a wildfire in the forest without any water, I was causing others to sin. According to Romans 5:19a in the King James Version "For as by one man's disobedience many were made sinners." This was referring to Adam in the Garden and how we became sinners, but we do the same thing when we cause others to sin.

   I got involved with a married man, who was also the pastor of a local church. He was younger than me and I never thought or wanted him to leave his wife, but he was willing to do it for me. When they say what goes around comes around is a true statement. Before repenting and asking for forgiveness, I got married and guess what? Yep, he cheated on me. I had to ask for forgives for what I had done in the past and asked God to help me get through it. It was hard, but I survived. Had I had an accountability partner like I have today I may not have gotten caught up in those things. It is said

misery loves company and when you are sinning you look for others to sin with you. I'm glad it did not stop there. God had a plan, an antidote for sin, Jesus. Romans

12:9 His grace is sufficient, and His strength is made known in our weakness, some versions say infirmities. He saved us by grace Ephesians 2:8, but we did not all get the same measure of grace Ephesians 4:7 says He gave you the amount of grace you needed for your sins and infirmities. Yours might not need as much as mine, but what I like about it, is that whatever amount you got was sufficient for you.

God is removing you from places, because you can't heal in the same place you got hurt. Don't get comfortable. He will heal you and send you back to where you were hurt as a testament of His glory.

Step Two: God will hear your cry *(your supplication) verses 8b -9a* You may think you have been in this thing too long and God doesn't hear you, I just heard Holy Spirit say, that's because of what people told you, not what God showed you. When you are down people, church folk are quick to tell you God won't hear you because of what you've been doing. Psalms 30:8 – "I cried to thee, O Lord; and unto the Lord I made supplication." This lets us know that

God hears us. I don't care how far you travel on your Damascus Road; God can arrest you at any time. Psalms 40:2 He lifted me out of a horrible pit of miry clay and set my feet on a rock to stand.

Once you get out, pray for those that helped you get to the pit and the ones you drug down there with you. Matthew 5:44 commands us to do so. We are commanded to love, so in order to heal your hurt you must learn how to love God's way. He heard your cry now you must hear the cry of others. Healing is a cleansing process, and we must follow the process. We must realize we cannot clean ourselves, but we need help. God tells us in Jeremiah 3:22 how to start the cleansing process. Return to Him and He will begin the healing process, we go to Him because He is our God, and He is the only one who can cleanse and heal us from you sin. He sent His son to die for us, Isaiah 53:5 tells us He was wounded for our transgressions and bruised for our iniquities the chastisement of our peace was upon Him, but by His stripes we are healed. The whipping He took on Calvary was not for himself, but it was for us. He was without sin, but He became sin and died for us that we might be saved.

So, when we fall short, He has already provided for us to come back to Him. He became hurt, so we could heal. He already took the punishment for us, so stop beating yourself up, Jesus paid the price not some, but all, so there is nothing you must do to start the healing process but return to Him and He will help you. I peter 4:8 lets us know that His love covers all sins.

Step Three: God will receive our prayers — in verse 9b & 10 God is going to set me

up in front of those who hurt me and make them be ashamed. That's good news. We do not have to take vengeance out on anyone because God is going to handle it. You don't even have to plot and plan; the plan has already been set. Your enemies will be ashamed and greatly troubled. When God heals you it's immediate and people will be astonished at His great works and be troubled. Acts 9:6 — Saul was astonished and trembling at what Christ had told him. It shook him so that it
turned his life around. God is waiting for you. Your healing is here. Your healing is

now. God wants to heal you from your hurt, so He can use you to build Heaven. I John 4:18 — start to love yourself don't be afraid, love cast our all fears. Try Jesus, give Him your fears, let Him take away the hurt and pain. You've been holding on too long, let it go! Give it to Him.

Understand that separation is not a bad thing. You see Jesus separated Himself from the disciples when He went to pray. We must learn how to pray in our hours of separation. This was the time He cried out to His Father and asked for direction. He cried tears of blood; this thing was serious. When you are into a thing you put your blood sweat and tears into it. Stop praying for it to work, because God may be trying to rid you of some things. Like Jesus, pray, Lord not my will, but Thy will be done. It may hurt, but removing things from your life will always hurt, but He had to for Him to complete His assignment and to heal. It's a process. Like any surgical removal you must allow the wound to hear. God is separating us to save us.

Reflections

How To Face Your Fears

Fear has its place in the world, but you do not have to be controlled by it. For many years after the death of my parents, I was paralyzed by fear. It was hard for me to move forward because I thought I would lose someone else close to me. Just recently, it dawned on me how much fear was controlling what I did. I can remember applying for jobs and trying to move to the next level in my educational career and my mom died, I stopped applying for jobs and became very stagnant. I also remember one summer day my son and I were riding bikes and I got the call that my father had died, seven months after my mom. Well, some 11 years later, I noticed I had not tried to advance in my career or ridden a bike since the news of their passing. I was not moving, so I sought the Lord and began a devotional study on overcoming fear, it was one of the best things I could have done. So, when my son's father passed, I was not afraid, it was an opportunity for me to exercise my faith and do what God had told me to do, MOVE! It may sound easy, but until you have faced fear head on and been paralyzed by the effects of it, you would not understand how difficult it is to do something as simple as moving. I took that leap of faith, packed up everything I owned, and my son and I set off for Colorado. There was no fear, just excitement of what God was about to do. I had a clean canvas to accomplish whatever He wanted me to do. Seven years there and I was hit with another faith move, I moved to Texas. I have been here three years now and God showed me in His word how to face every fear without fear.

Psalm 27:1-4 "The Lord is my light and my salvation, whom shall I fear? The Lord is the strength of my life; of whom shall I be afraid? When the wicked, even mine enemies and my foes, came upon me to eat up my flesh. They stumble and fell. Though a host should encamp against me, my heart shall not fear: Though war should rise against me, in this will I be confident. One thing I desired of the Lord, that will I seek after; That I may dwell in the house of the Lord all the days of my life, to behold the beauty of the Lord, and to enquire in his temple."

When we understand not only who we are, but whose we are, we can combat the spirit of fear. We were not given a spirit of fear, but of a sound mind and power. When facing your fears know who you belong too.

In verse 1 it says, the Lord is the strength of my life, in this verse Lord in the Hebrew is Donay, meaning a title of the one true God, with focus on His majesty and authority. We belong to the one true God, and we walk in His authority. We can honestly stand on the fact that Greater is He who is in us than he who is in the world. If your problem is no greater than raising Jesus from the dead, you do not have a problem that He cannot fix.

    The word salvation in this passage means Yesa, in the Hebrew it means deliverance, protection, often employing a victory is at hand. So why should we fear anything when our Heavenly Father has already ensured we have victory through our faith is in Him and He has a good track record when it comes to victories. Jesus conquered death, hell and the grave, so what makes you think he is afraid to tackle anything you are dealing with. Again, know whose you are, we are joint heirs with Christ and have access to the throne of God just as He does. Salvation rescued us from earthly enemies, often referring to our salvation from guilt, sin, and punishment, we are saved and safe from those things that would otherwise take us out.

Now to deal with the word fear, what is fear? I'm glad you asked, fear is yare in

Hebrew, which means to be terrified, frightened, intimidated. We do need to understand there is a difference between fearing things and/or people and fearing God. Fearing people can leave you wondering if you are worthy, able or capable to proceed in life. When fearing God, it gives Him reference and respect. The scripture says that demons tremble in fear when they see Him. We have the same power within us to combat anything that will come up against us. There
was a time when the power went out and millions were without power, now I'm not

saying that the other people did not pray or did not know the Lord, but we must stop thinking these companies hold all the power. My power went out for the evening and when I woke the next morning, I called on a higher power. I prayed and blessed and anointed my house and asked the Power of the Holy Spirit that was like fire shut up in my bones to heat my house and touch the powers that be to restore the power in my house. I went to the grocery store to get some food and upon my return the electricity was on and stayed on through the duration of the storm. Those of you in Texas, know exactly which storm I am talking about, the one that shut down Texas shut down because of an ice storm. We must start believing what God shows us about ourselves and pray in faith. We do not have to walk in fear. We must stop giving our power to things that are powerless.

Next, do not render yourself powerless. Know your battle stance. Know how to fight the things you are coming up against. The scripture says, we wrestle not against flesh and blood but principalities of darkness in high places. Some of us do not have the battle stance to fight these demons. You cannot go to a gun fight with a knife or with your bare hands. Equip yourself for the battle. There is a war cry, there is an alarm that will sound. When you face your fears, seek the Lord, inquire of Him, sit with Him. He will remove you from the enemies' scope while He prepares you.

Finally, you will have a brand-new awakening. You'll be able to walk around and sing of His goodness. Understand when we praise God during our hard times Satan gets mad. So, when you are facing your fears, praise God and watch what He does.

God is always there in our darkest hour. Ask Jesus, when it got dark and He gave up the Ghost, He cried its's finished and the Father came to His rescue. It may appear that He has forsaken us, but that is when He is working to hide us. After He finishes hiding us, then He will present you faultless. Remember when facing your fears that the Bible tells us in 2 Timothy 1:7 – For God hath not given us the spirit of fear; but of power, and of love and of a sound mind. Keep your mind stayed on

Jesus and He will keep you in perfect peace. Be not swayed by every wind and doctrine, but be ye steadfast, unmovable and always abounding in the Lord.

Keep these truths every before you and you will not go wrong, and you will be able to face every fear with victory.

Reflections

Relevance After Rejection

Rejection can be a hard pill to swallow, especially from those who are closest to you and know you. But what do you do when you are rejected by people before they even get a chance to know who you are? You walk in a room and people are looking at you funny and you do not have a clue as to why. Well, nine times out of ten someone in the room has said something about you before you got there. Well, chin up because you are in good company. They have a saying that says, there is nothing new under the sun. Well, it is true, Jesus went through the same thing, He was judged before the people even got a chance to know Him. You know how they say your reputation proceeds you, it is true, because John the Baptist made the announcement loud and clear that He was coming. So, consider yourself privileged to be in the same company as Jesus. After all the scriptures said we would suffer greater things than He, so do not be too surprised by the things that happen to you.

In Psalms 118:22 tells us that Jesus was rejected by the builders before they knew who He was and what He was going to be, He is the chief cornerstone, the anchor to hold up the building. You see man will reject things that they do not understand, but all things are not meant for them to understand, nor will they understand the ways of God without His explanation. Men will reject you so many ways until it has you thinking you are no good for anything. One all have been rejected at some point and time in our lives, but we must understand that rejection is not the end. This is not the time to crawl into a corner, or under a rock and die. The best things must be rejected before they can be refined. When the potter works on his clay it does not always come out right the first time, it may be flawed or have an air pocket in it. It cannot be repaired, so it must be broken down before they can start over. It is not easy to fix something with a lot of worth with just a patch on the area that is in question. But as the potter begins, they can see what happened and where they need to apply more clay next time. You must literally destroy the piece and start over from scratch. Diamonds go through a similar process. When you get diamonds, they do not come formed they come in pieces that have to be heated, buffed, filed and chipped away at. This does not achieve a rare diamond on the first try, but it must be repeated until you get a diamond that is flawless.

 All things including humans must be shaped and molded in a process that may take more than once to get to the desired outcome. Once the desired outcome is achieved you will have a refined and relevant piece of work ready to present to the world. It may now be placed on display to be admired by on lookers and ready to go home with someone. Have you ever been broken? Thought that you were not anymore good to anyone? Left for dead so to speak? Thought, Is this the end? Trust me you are not alone. We have all been in those positions at some point and time in our lives. It is all in how you handle it that will determine how long your refining process will take. If you submit early and often, it may not take as long as it would for someone who is stubborn and wants to do it all their way or it is the highway, remove yourself from that and begin to rebuild yourself. What have you gone through?

Reflections

How To Build

1 Peter 2:1-8 King James Version, gives us the steps to take to build with rejected stones. Verse 1 reads, wherefore laying aside all malice, and all guile, and hypocrisies, and envies, and all evil speaking, when you lay something aside you get rid of it, put it away it is dead to you know, so what do we do with dead things? You bury them, so you need to have a funeral with all the old things that have happened that caused your stones to be rejected. Anytime you hold on to malice, guile hypocrisies, envy and evil

speech you cause more issues for yourself. These are the things that cause most people stress and anxiety.

These are things you cannot see, but they do not show signs on the outside, they are manifesting on the inside. When you get rid of these things you can begin to remold who you are and begin again. So many times, we know what is hindering us from moving forward and we want to hold on to it. The longer we hold on to things that have rejected us or broken us down the longer it takes to rebuild.

To rebuild you must face all

the things that have rejected you otherwise you will build with faulty materials, and it will fall apart again and again.

Like the potter, when he starts over, he does not use the same mold, he starts over. Jesus was rejected, but he did not hold on to what was said about Him,
He put it aside and died for us anyway. You many say what does that have to do with anything. Well, Jesus was rejected by those He came to save and set free, but they did not believe He was the Messiah and they rejected Him, but he just put

those things behind Him and moved on, which is what we need to do.

Once you have laid things aside you have become as a newborn baby, you get the chance to start over without the mistakes, verse 2-3 (KJV) says, as newborn babes, desire the sincere milk of the work, that ye may grow thereby: if so be ye have tasted that the Lord is gracious. So now that you have been allowed to get rid of some things it is time
to start doing things different, you can no longer do things the way you use to. Being new you should desire to be different.

The things you use to do you do not do anymore. The places you use to go you do not go anymore, especially if that is what rejected you the first time.

Why would you want to go back to the people or places that rejected you? Well, you should not, at least not until you are strong enough to handle it. I am not saying you will not want to; I am just saying get strong first. Too many times we try to go back to the people and places that rejected us before we are healed, and we get hurt even more because we were not ready.

Your appetite and desires will begin to develop for something else and you will begin to appreciate what you have and understand that He knows what you are going through because He went through it. He was rejected and despised, by men, but God.

See people may reject you and speak all manner of things against you, but God. Once you have moved away you can start to become what God wants you to be. A house not made by mans' hands. The Father takes the rejected stones and molds them into spiritual buildings, the pieces are all shapes and sizes, but He knows exactly where they fit. As you begin to get fitted those that rejected you will begin to stumble over your beauty and what you can do.

You will begin to love those who rejected you and you will begin to heal, love and forgive the way Christ did. Stop hiding the new building.

Now you are ready to present the new you and take your proper placement. You see just because you were once rejected did not mean you were discarded. Most would like to think that a reject does not work. Quite the contrary, a reject may still work, but it has some cliches in it from time to time. It is just like a car you may purchase. It runs fine and you do not see any problems, but one day you get a letter in the mail saying there is a recall on your car because of something on it was rejected and you need to bring it into the shop to have it repaired. Well, they did not say you had to get rid of the whole car, you just need to bring it in so they may replace the rejected part then you may go. Same way with us, we may be broken but the Father wants you to come in for a healing tune-up to get you back to running the way you need to. The Bible tells us that, the race is not given to the swift or the strong, but to the one who endures until the end. Keep pressing, keep praying and keep producing.

Reflections

Victory Is Mine

Wow! Betrayal, I bet you did not see that one coming? How many of you have been betrayed by someone? How many of those persons were close to you? There is victory after this.

Most times we get upset with the person with whom we have been betrayed when we find out we have been betrayed, but should we? Well let's see the definition according to the Webster's Online dictionary the word betrayal is **'an act of deliberate disloyalty.'** Then I looked up deliberate. Well deliberate means done consciously and intentionally. Then you have victory, victory means, an act of defeating an enemy or opponent in a battle, game, or other competition.

Most people think that betrayal comes from people you do not know but based on the definition it could not possibly be. It said it was someone who was disloyal. Well, I do not know about you, but I do not have too many enemies that are loyal to me, unless you count them being dedicated to hating me. You can truly say that 9 times out of 10 your betrayer is someone close to you. Someone you know and they know you. We must understand that we already know who our betrayers are.

Understand, to be betrayed they must first be loyal to you. The ultimate demonstration of betrayal came in John 13:21, when Jesus was having His last supper with the disciples. Jesus had been with his disciples for some time, and He knew them personally, they were close to Him, but He knew that there was one among them that was going to betray Him. Jesus did not treat Him any different, the disciples wanted to know who it was, but He did not tell them, He addressed Judas without anyone knowing what He said.

We must learn from this example and be able to identify our betrayers and let them know that we know who they are without telling them. You cannot be surprised when they are revealed. Jesus did not go off, He just addressed him amid His inner circle.

You may be asking, Why Jesus did not call him out? If I could answer that with my Super-Natural mind, I would say Jesus did not have to address him by name, because

His betrayer also knew who he was. See not only do you already know who your betrayer is, but they also know who they are and what they set out to do. Most people in your circle attach to you for different reasons and one of them is for notoriety and if betraying you will get them that, you better believe they will do it.

Another reason could be to destroy you, which is what Judas thought he would be doing. After Jesus broke bread he said the next one He feed would be the one to betray Him. He dipped the bread and gave it to Judas to eat and the scripture said Satan immediately entered him and Jesus told him to go do what he needed to do and do it quickly (John 13:27).

In getting victory from betrayal, you must know how to release your betrayer. As you see Jesus did not embarrass Judas, but He whispered in his ear what He had to say. He released him to go and do what he needed to do. Our biggest problem is, when it is time to identify our betrayer, we want to call them out and embarrass them in front of other people., when that is not the example set by Christ. We always say we want to be more Christ like, but we do not want to follow His examples.

　　Letting your betrayer go must be a smooth transition as if nothing has happened, not to alarm others that something is happening. Jesus was smooth in releasing Judas, He whispered in his ear what he needed to do, the other disciples thought Jesus gave him a task to do, nothing out of the ordinary because he was the treasure. Now this should let you know that your betrayer even has a good position in your camp, they are not someone just sitting idly by, remember it is always someone close to you. Someone who was once loyal to you because, only someone who has been loyal to you can be deliberately disloyal. I hope this is making sense. Being betrayed is not something one is proud to tell so when it happens, take the steps needed to ensure healing.

The final step to help you have victory after a betrayal is knowing you will receive glory afterwards. John 13:31 says, that after Judas left, Jesus said, "Now the son of Man is glorified, and God is glorified in Him. The things we go through is not about us, but it is for the glory of God and

by giving Him glory, He will glorify us with Him, but we must follow His lead, not go out on a tangent, and do what we want. So many times, we do not get healed because we mess up the steps to healing from the betrayal. We must give God time to do what it is He is going to do. For us to fulfill our greatest potential
we must humble ourselves. Jesus humbled Himself for us and came down to die for our sins. He was a man who had done no wrong and He was crucified, and betrayed by those who were to love Him, so imagine what your friends and loved ones will do

to you. The scripture says, we will be persecuted for His name's sake, and we would suffer greater things. If we suffer in Him and for Him, we will get the glory afterwards. The race is not given to the swift or the strong, but to the one that endures until the end. This is a promise from God, and He is not like man that He would tell a lie but fulfill it util the day of Christ. Get your healing and receive your glory

Reflections

My Brother's Keeper

So many times, we get upset when we are corrected, but we are told to watch out for one another, and not just spiritually. We also get offended when we are corrected on our job, at church, or at school. You miss a deadline and think no one is supposed to say anything. Oh, but when they do you want to throw a whole fit. The Bible says to work as unto God. How are you honoring God by missing deadlines, and due dates? Oh, I forgot we don't follow order when it comes to God. We show up late for minister's meeting, and choir rehearsal, we don't do the homework that was assigned, we don't give, I know we don't want to hear this kind of stuff, because it hurts, that's why it's called correction.

Why is it we only have a problem with correction when it comes from a ministry leader? The respect that we give our spiritual leaders is ridiculous, we question them more, we disrespect them more, we don't follow directions and we wonder why the church is messed up. In life we must check ourselves daily and do some self-correction as well as being accountable to someone else so we can also be corrected by others.

Galatians 6:1 Brethren, if a man is overtaken in any trespass, you who are spiritual restore such a one in a spirit of gentleness, considering yourself lest you also be tempted. We must understand that the word man here is not just talking about a gender, but all mankind. The scriptures say, for all have sinned and fallen short of His glory, that means you too, and overtaken means something has caught up with you while going in the same direction. I know that may be a little

confusing. It means something of misfortune comes upon you suddenly or unexpectedly. When you are overtaken by a thing, you did not see it coming. Some trespasses we know are eventually coming because of the things we have done, but this scripture is speaking of things out of the realm of your control. You can be accountable for things you know you are doing, but how do you
hold yourself accountable for something you had no part in, but it is now sitting in your lap, and you must deal with it? Now it's time for you to be willing to be

corrected by your brother or sister. In being your brother's keeper, there are some key things that we must keep in mind for this process to be successful for all especially the fallen one.

Being ready to restore is a key, being empathic to people is the ability to understand a person's state of mind, state of being, both mental and psychological. So many times, we dismiss people based on what we see on the outside, not knowing that what is seen on the outside is because of a manifestation of something else on the inside. People may not always express how they feel, but if you are attentive enough you will be able to read signs and see red flags when people are not being truthful. Not because they want to lie, but because they may be ashamed or embarrassed by what it is they are going through. Outward appearance does not always dictate outer expression, usually it is the other way around.

If we want to be helpful, we also must be gentle with people when we are correcting them. Speaking to them like a warden is not going to make them want to open up to you. My mom used to say, "You can get more with honey than you can with vinegar." In other words, be nice to people instead of being nasty. Most times it is not what you say, but how you say it. Being an English teacher, I teach about tone, inflection, mood, perception, connotation and denotation, all of these are a part of the English language, and they play a part in how you may come across to another person during a conversation. Some things you say, you may not mean it the way they perceived it, but that is how they interpreted what was said, and that's what matters. You speak to people based on past experiences with a situation, this is your connotation and denotation which causes you to feel good or bad about it. This determines if you want to help or not as well.

You must meet people where they are, as the scripture said, he who is mature in the Lord should help those who are not. So, you cannot assume that they will be receptive to what you have to say. We must learn how to be conscious of people's state of mind and what they may be going through at the time. There is a reason for everything that we do, so try to find out what that is, if you make them feel comfortable and at ease, they may be willing to speak with you about their situation.

Being ready to bare some burdens is another way to heal through correction. You must be willing to take responsibility for your actions and to help others realize their part. Galatians 6:2 says, we should bare one another's burdens, that means we are not just accountable for ourselves. Some people do not even know when they have done wrong. They believe that everything they are doing is right, hence why people continue to sin because they do not feel they are doing anything wrong.

Give people a safe space to be able to talk about what they have done. The "Church" is so quick to turn their backs on people when they fall short, and they forget that they were once in that same position and possibly can be there at any moment. Galatians 6:3 says, For if anyone thinks himself to be something, when he is nothing, he deceives himself. Having a safe space to vent without judgement can be the difference between life and death for some.

Always being ready to examine yourself will help with correction. That accountability piece is key in recovering from making mistakes Galatians 6:4 — tells us to examine ourselves and the work we have done, when we do that, we do not have time to worry about what someone else is doing. I like to say, "It takes six months for me to mind my own business and six months for me to leave someone else alone. Therefore, I do not have time to worry about making fun of the mistakes you are making, because I am making my own. In minding your own business, you will be able to acknowledge the accomplishments you have made, celebrating your accomplishments no matter how great or small is going to help you have self-confidence, self-esteem, and a better character analysis of yourself. Self-awareness will help you go a long way. It will help you with the confidence you need to be a strong, independent person. Don't allow fear to keep you bound.

Reflections

Time To Go

During our healing process we must be able to hear from God. I know what you are thinking, that's hard, and your right it is hard to hear from God when you are going through, when you are hurting, when you feel betrayed, when you feel like there is no one there, but you. Sometimes when we get hurt or continue to get hurt because we leave a place to soon or we stay too long. They say sin will take you places you don't want to go and keep you longer than you want to stay, but we must get strong enough to know when it is time to go.

When we are healing from hurting situations, we need to know when it is time to go. This reminds me of Matthew 2:20-23 the story of King Herod trying to get rid of Jesus. God knew what was going on, so He went to Joseph and gave him instructions. You must know that the things you are going through are not about you, but about the God you serve. Satan is made that you are even alive because he knows what you are capable of. That is why he is trying to get rid of your baby. Not a physical baby, but the assignments, the ideas, the creativity, that God is trying to birth out of you. Someone is trying to keep you from birthing them. Just as King Herod was trying to keep Jesus from being born, but God.

God has spoken to you in a dream and told you what to do, where to go, when to go, and how long
to stay there just like He did Joseph when Mary was pregnant with baby Jesus. The key is to make sure you hear God's voice and stay as long as He tells you. Sometimes we move prematurely and that is not could

when it comes to birthing, you do not want a vision or

assignment to come out prematurely because it may be killed if it comes too early. Sometimes our own thoughts can play tricks on us, and we start to believe what we tell ourselves and don't believe what God said and try to do our own thing and during it all God steps in and reveals something to you that could be potentially harmful or detrimental to you if you don't listen to what He said.

    This message will cause you to change your plans. I know you're probably thinking, but I already told everyone what I was doing, and they are going look at me funny if I change now. Well, do you want to do what God said and please Him, or follow your plan and please man? Listen to God and watch what happens.

In Matthew 2:22- It has already been prophesied as to where you are supposed to be. Don't miss your blessing because you wanted to be hardheaded and stick to your own agenda. God is not like man He will not lie, if He said it, you could bet your bottom dollar you can believe it. When you reach your appointed place,
may your dreams will be fulfilled.

Reflections

Postlude

God rescue from myself, release me from my past hurt. If this sounds like you repeat after me if you're struggling with your past and say, Lord help me to let go of my past, help me to forgive those who hurt me, so I may have total healing, help me to see me as you see me. Help me to break the past agreements that do not line up with what You said about me. The scripture says, If my people who are called by My name, would humble themselves and pray, seek my face and turn from their wicked ways, I will hear from Heaven and heal their land. So it is, it is so, Amen.

Now when we pray, we want to end that with a declaration and a decree. I decree and declare to all of you reading this right now, that those things that hurt you in the past will not determine your future. Starting right now you are set free, for whom the Son set free is free indeed. I decree and declare this is your new beginning, you are FREE!

www.ingramcontent.com/pod-product-compliance
Lightning Source LLC
Chambersburg PA
CBHW071906070526
44583CB00016B/1871